"The older I grow, the more I am personally convinced that the church is our Lord's answer to the adopting of so many precious children who so desperately are in need of a good home. Dr. Russell Moore has done the church a tremendous service by reminding us in this writing of the call of God to meet the ever-pressing needs of these little ones. Read with the intent to obey."

Johnny Hunt, Former President, The Southern Baptist Convention; Senior Pastor, First Baptist Church Woodstock, Woodstock, Georgia

"Russell Moore shows how churches should view adoption as part of their mission. He shows what a difference it would make if Christians were known once again as the people who take in orphans and make them sons and daughters."

Marvin Olasky, Editor in Chief, World News Group

"This is a powerfully insightful book of how adoption is a beautiful act of love and mission for the gospel. I pray that God uses this book to encourage and impact many, many lives."

Dan Kimball, Pastor, Vintage Faith Church; author, *They Like Jesus but Not the Church*

"This book is for all who have been adopted by God. Moore illumines the beauty and wonder of our adoption in Christ and its profound and necessary implications for orphan care and the earthly practice of adoption. If you want to deepen your worship of the God who adopts and who has revealed himself to be a "Father to the fatherless," *Adoption* will serve you exceptionally well."

Dan Cruver, Director, Together for Adoption; author, *Reclaiming Adoption: Missional Living Through the Rediscovery of Abba Father*

"The Bible tells us that pure religion is caring for widows and orphans. Dr. Russell Moore challenges Christians to an aspect of Christ's lordship that many have never considered. His remarkable way of putting our salvation into the context of being adopted into God's family brings a new perspective on being the recipient of undeserved mercy and grace."

Jerry Rankin, Former President, International Mission Board of the Southern Baptist Convention

Adoption

What Joseph of Nazareth Can Teach Us
about This Countercultural Choice

Russell Moore

CROSSWAY

WHEATON, ILLINOIS

Adoption: What Joseph of Nazareth Can Teach Us about This Countercultural Choice

Copyright © 2015 by Russell D. Moore

Published by Crossway
        1300 Crescent Street
        Wheaton, Illinois 60187

First published as "Joseph of Nazareth vs. Planned Parenthood: What's at Stake When We Talk about Adoption," chapter 3 in *Adopted for Life* (Crossway), copyright 2009 by Russell D. Moore, pp. 59–84.

Cover design: Tim Green, Faceout Studio

Cover image: Getty Images

First printing 2015

Printed in the United States of America

Trade paperback ISBN: 978-1-4335-4991-5
ePub ISBN: 978-1-4335-4994-6
PDF ISBN: 978-1-4335-4992-2
Mobipocket ISBN: 978-1-4335-4993-9

Library of Congress Cataloging-in-Publication Data

Moore, Russell, 1971–
   Adoption : what Joseph of Nazareth can teach us about this
countercultural choice / Russell D. Moore.
     pages cm
   Includes bibliographical references.
   ISBN 978-1-4335-4991-5 (pbk.)
   1. Joseph, Saint. 2. Adoption—Religious aspects—
Christianity. 3. Bible—Criticism, interpretation, etc. I. Title.
BS2458.M66   2015
261.8'35874—dc23   2014046491

Crossway is a publishing ministry of Good News Publishers.

BP		25	24	23	22	21	20	19	18	17	16	15
15	14	13	12	11	10	9	8	7	6	5	4	3	2	1

To the Highview Baptist Church
in Louisville, Kentucky, and the
Kingdom First Bible Study class.
I am enriched every day by memories
of the years serving with you.

Contents

Preface

What it would mean if our churches and families were known as the people who adopt babies—and toddlers, and children, and teenagers. What if we as Christians were known, once again, as the people who take in orphans, and make of them beloved sons and daughters?

Not everyone is called to adopt. No one wants parents who adopt children out of the same sense of duty with which they may give to the building fund for the new church gymnasium. But all of us have a stake in the adoption issue, because Jesus does. He is the one who tells us his Father is also the "Father of the fatherless" (Ps. 68:5). He is the One who insists on calling "the least of these" his brothers (Matt. 25:40), and who tells us that the first time we hear his voice he will be asking us if we did the same.

I don't know why, in the mystery of God's plan, you were led to pick up this booklet. But,

I know this. You have a stake in the adoption issue—even if you never adopt a child. There's a war going on around you—and perhaps within you—and adoption is one crucial arena of that war. With that in mind, perhaps there are some changes to be made in our lives. For some of us, I hope this book changes the makeup of our households. For some of us, I hope it helps to change our monthly bank account balances. For all of us, I hope it changes something of the way we say "brother" and "sister" in our pews next Sunday, and the way we cry out "Father" on our knees tonight.

Joseph of Nazareth

What's at Stake When We Talk about Adoption

I played a cow in my first-grade Christmas pageant, and I had more lines than the kid who played Joseph. He was a prop, or so it seemed, for Mary, the plastic doll in the manger, and the rest of us. We were just following the script. There's rarely much room in the inn of the contemporary Christian imagination for Joseph, especially among conservative Protestants like me. His only role, it seems, is an usher—to get Mary to the stable in Bethlehem in the first place and then to get her back to the Temple in Jerusalem in order to find the wandering twelve-year-old Jesus.

But there's much more to the Joseph figure.

Joseph serves as a model to follow as we see what's at stake in the issue of adoption. Joseph, after all, is an adoptive father. In some ways, his situation is, of course, far different from that of any reader holding this book right now. In other ways, though, Joseph's mission belongs to all of us. As Joseph images the Father of the fatherless, he shows us how adoption is more than charity. It's spiritual warfare.

1

Adoption and Spiritual Warfare

The couple looked familiar to me as I saw them approaching, smiling, pushing a stroller toward me, but I couldn't place their names. It was the annual summer meeting of my denomination, so I was used to renewing old acquaintances from all over the country. The husband was the first to speak, and he told me that he and his wife had met with me about adoption a few years earlier when they were students at the seminary I served. They wanted me to see the little boy they had adopted, from a former Soviet state. I knelt down to talk with the little fellow as he shyly curled back in his seat. The little boy had beautiful olive skin coloring, looked as though he had Arabic or perhaps Persian roots, and had cute little chubby cheeks. As I played peekaboo with the little boy, I asked the parents if they'd had any trouble with bureaucracy along the way.

"The only problem we had was with the judge," the wife said. "The judge thought there was some mistake that we'd want this child because he's dark skinned. The judge said no one would want a child like that and that there were plenty of light-skinned babies available. He just couldn't believe that we would want him and almost treated us as though we were up to something shady because we did."

I wasn't expecting that, and as I stroked this little boy's cheek, those words struck me: "No one would ever want a child like that." I picked him up from his stroller and hugged him, hoping I wouldn't start crying in front of my denominational peers walking up and down the corridor of the convention hall. "You're loved and wanted," I told him. "Isn't that great?"

After I finished the conversation with the family and went back to the relative inanity of voting on resolutions and motions on the convention floor, I couldn't get the horror of that situation off my mind. How could a judge sit in his chair and deem that lovable child to be unworthy of love simply because of the shade of his skin? What kind of backward Philistines were they dealing with in that courtroom?

And then I remembered that my denomination, in whose deliberations I then sat, was formed in a dispute with other American Christians over the slavery of other human beings because of the color of their skin. And my people had been on the slaveholders' side. Previous generations of preachers just like me (indeed probably some related to me) had argued that some children were unworthy of freedom because of the shade of their skin. My own ancestors had seen to it that children of a darker skin than themselves were made orphans. As the resolutions flew around the convention hall about "the sanctity of marriage," I realized that previous generations of preachers in this very same context had propped up a system in which parents couldn't marry legally because that would make it more difficult to sell them individually when necessary.

A similar story could be told a billion times over in virtually every human society throughout history. There seems to be an orphan-making urge among us, whether we see it in the slave culture of centuries past or the divorce culture of today. But where does it come from?

The Rage of Pharaoh, Herod, and Planned Parenthood

In the stories preserved for us by Jesus's disciples Matthew and Luke, we see that Joseph of Nazareth discovers something of the root behind it all. Joseph, after all, finds himself a player in a story that has played out before.

The Gospel of Matthew tells us that King Herod learns from some traveling stargazers that the foreseen birth of the royal son of David is here. Herod is "troubled, and all Jerusalem with him" (Matt. 2:3). Herod pores over the ancient scrolls, not in order to submit to them in faith, but to see how to circumvent this new king. Herod is right, of course. The promised Anointed One is a threat to Herod's tyranny. The son of David will receive, God has promised, a galactic empire with all his enemies under his feet. Herod protects his position through infanticide. He orders all the male children under two in the region of Bethlehem, the prophesied location of the Davidic king's birth, to be executed by royal decree.

Herod surely didn't think about the fact that he was playing the role of Pharaoh, but he was. This scenario is precisely what had played out thousands of years before when another ruler had his power threatened by the offspring of Abraham.

In the writings of Moses, we see that the Egyptian king saw the people of Israel among his population, that they "were fruitful and increased greatly; they multiplied and grew exceedingly strong, so that the land was filled with them" (Ex. 1:7).

Notice that this description of the Israelites is precisely what God has defined already as blessing. God promises at the creation that he will bless the man and the woman by making them fruitful, multiplying them across the face of the earth (Gen. 1:28). God blesses Abraham by promising to make him fruitful and to multiply his offspring to be as many as the stars of the sky (Gen. 15:5; 17:6).

What God pronounces as blessing, Pharaoh sees as a curse. Why? Pharaoh is worshiping the self as god, and the multiplication of the Hebrew people is a threat to the power of this god. So he seeks to remove that threat by any means necessary. First, he tries oppression, then the murder of infants.

Years later, Herod is another Pharaoh. The blessing of all blessings—the coming of the Christ—is seen by Herod in starkly personal terms. If there was an occupant on David's throne, it meant Herod wouldn't be "King of the Jews" anymore. And that just couldn't be, so he lashed out in murderous rage.

What's noteworthy about both Pharaoh and Herod is that both of them represent nations raging against God's Christ (Ps. 2:1–2). In Pharaoh's case, his rage is against the mass of Abraham's descendants, but this is a multitude that God pronounces as his "firstborn son" (Ex. 4:22–23). God knows that it was this people, in the fullness of time, from whom he will bring forth his Christ. If Pharaoh exterminated this people group, the consequences would be even greater than genocide; the consequences would be hell for the entire world. Herod knew full well what the old prophecies said about the Messiah. He probably prayed ornate prayers that God would send his promised king in the last days. But when the last days were suddenly upon him, Herod hated Jesus, even just by reputation.

What's also noteworthy about both of these dictators is that both of them take the rage they had against Jesus in particular and direct it toward babies in general. When it's Jesus versus the self, babies are caught in the crossfire. And it's always that way. Several years ago a friend sent me a copy of what just might be the most chilling Christmas card ever sent through the US mail. The Planned Parenthood Federation of America, the nation's leading provider of abortions, unveiled a holiday greeting card in support of the group's commitment to "reproductive freedom." The card was beautifully designed, complete with embossed snowflakes and stars made of glitter. Across the card was the caption, "Choice on Earth."

Across the country, evangelicals and Roman Catholics and others were outraged. In terms of in-your-face religious hostility, that card can only be compared to a Hanukkah card featuring a menorah twisted into a swastika. How could an organization devoted to something that orthodox Christians of every tradition in every generation have abhorred turn a phrase from the Christian Scripture into a fund-raising event for their cause?

It turns out, though, that the Planned Parenthood greeting card is quite appropriate for the time of year when Christians celebrate the incarnation. We ought to be reminded that Jesus is not born into a gauzy, snowy winter wonderland of sweetly singing angels and cute reindeer nuzzling one another at the side of his manger. He is born into a war zone. And at the very rumor of his coming, Herod—the Planned

Parenthood of his day—vows to see him dead, right along with thousands of his brothers.

Again, it's always that way. The Bible tells us so. Whether through political machinations such as those of Pharaoh and Herod, through military conquests in which bloodthirsty armies rip babies from pregnant mothers' wombs (Amos 1:13), or through the more "routine"-seeming family disintegration and family chaos, children are always hurt. Human history is riddled with their corpses.

Satan's Rage against Christ and Children

Why? It's because there are not just impersonal economic and sociological factors at work. "The course of this world" is driven along by "the prince of the power of the air" (Eph. 2:2). Jesus showed his disciple John what the story behind the story is. It's the picture of a woman giving birth to "a male child, one who is to rule all the nations with a rod of iron" (Rev. 12:5). Crouching before this woman's birth canal is a dragon, the Serpent of old, who seeks to "devour" the baby (Rev. 12:4). That dragon then "became furious with the woman and went off to make war on the rest of her offspring" (Rev. 12:17) and has done so ever since.

The demonic powers hate babies because they hate Jesus. When they destroy "the least of these" (Matt. 25:40, 45), the most vulnerable among us, they're destroying a picture of Jesus himself, of the child delivered by the woman who crushes their head (Gen. 3:15). They know the human race is saved—and they're vanquished—by a woman giving birth (Gal. 4:4; 1 Tim. 2:15). They are grinding apart Jesus's brothers and sisters (Matt. 25:40). They are also destroying the very picture of newness of life and of dependent trust that characterizes life in the kingdom of Christ (Matt. 18:4). Children also mean blessing—a perfect target for those who seek only to kill and destroy (John 10:10).

The demonic powers are, we must remember, rebel angels—angels created to be "ministering spirits sent out to serve for the sake of those who are to inherit salvation" (Heb. 1:14). In rebelling against this calling, the servants are in revolt against the sons, and that kind of insurrection leads to murder, as we've seen in other contexts (e.g., Mark 12:1–12). As James tells us, our lust for things we can't have leads to wars among us (James 4:2). The same is true in the heavenly places. The satanic powers want the kingdoms of the universe—

and a baby uproots their reign. So they rage all the more against the babies and children who image him. As the wisdom of God announces, "All who hate me love death" (Prov. 8:36).

Satan always uses human passions to bring about his purposes. When new life stands in the way of power—whether that power is a Pharaoh's military stability or a community leader's reputation in light of his teenage daughter's pregnancy—the blood of children often flows. Herod loved his power, so he raged against babies. In the middle of all of this stood Joseph, an unlikely demon wrestler.

Defending Children Despite the Disruption

It's easy to shake our heads in disgust at Pharaoh or Herod or Planned Parenthood. It's not as easy to see the ways in which we ourselves often have a Pharaoh-like view of children rather than a Christlike view.[1] What God calls blessing, we often grumble at as a curse—and for the same reason those old kings did, because they disrupt our life plans. Our "kingdom" may be smaller than that of those old kings, our pyramids and monuments less enduring; but it's all still there. I'm not arguing that parents should have as many children as biologically possible. I'm not arguing that every family is called to adopt children.

I am suggesting, though, that we look at some of the ways in which we refuse to see blessing in something as noisy and frustrating as a child. Just last night I huffed around my house, sullen with anger. My son Timothy had accidentally spilled milk on a notebook full of notes for this chapter. He apologized, and I accepted his apology, but I had that look in my eyes and that angry setting to my mouth. It wasn't until this morning that the Spirit convicted me of harboring anger toward a little child, all because he innocently disrupted my plans—my plans to, of all things, write a book about the glory of adoption. What a hypocrite. Children disrupt plans, and blessedly so. They might disrupt yours. It's easy to resent this disruption and lash out against it, perhaps not in murder but in the anger that's the root of murder (Matt. 5:21–22).

It might be that you're reading this book because your spouse wants to adopt, and you're arguing you can't afford it. Maybe you're right. But could it be the Lord is calling you to adopt, and you know you can't "afford" it while maintaining the stuff you have right now? It might be you're reading this book because your son or daughter wants to adopt, and you're thinking about talking them out of it. It's just so expensive, or it's just not the right time. Maybe you're right. But maybe you're just not seeing what's at stake here.

The protection of children isn't charity. It isn't part of a political program fitting somewhere between tax cuts and gun rights or between carbon emission caps and a national service corps. It's spiritual warfare.

Our God forbids Israel from offering their children to Molech, a demon-god who demands the violent sacrifice of human babies (Lev. 20:1–5). Indeed, he denounces Molech by name. He further warns that he will cut off from the people of God not only the one who practiced such sacrifice but also all who "at all close their eyes to that man when he gives one of his children to Molech" (Lev. 20:4). Behind Molech, God recognizes, there is one who is "a murderer from the beginning" (John 8:44).

The spirit of Molech is at work among us even now. Even as you read this page, there are bones of babies being ground to unrecognizable bits, perhaps even a few short miles from where you're sitting. There are babies lying in garbage receptacles waiting to be taken away as "medical waste." These infants won't have names until Jesus calls them out for the first time. There are little girls waiting in Asia for a knock at the door, for an American business-man who's paid a pimp to be able to sexually assault them. There are children staring out the window of a social worker's office, rubbing their bruises as they hear their mother tell the police why she'll never do it again.

Aborted babies can't say, "*Abba.*" But the Father hears their cries anyway. Do we?

The universe is at war, and some babies and children are on the line. The old Serpent is coiled right now, his tongue flicking, watching for infants and children he can consume. One night two thousand years ago, all that stood in his way was one reluctant day laborer who decided to be a father.

2

Adoption and the Image of God

When we talk about Joseph at all, we spend most of our time talking about what he was *not*. We believe (rightly) with the apostles that Jesus was conceived in a virgin's womb. Joseph was not Jesus's biological father; not a trace of Joseph's sperm was involved in the formation of the embryo Christ. No amount of Joseph's DNA could be found in the dried blood of Jesus peeled from the wood of Golgotha's cross. Jesus was conceived by the Holy Spirit completely apart from the will or exertion of any man.

Joseph's Role as Adoptive Father

That noted, though, we need to be careful that we don't reduce Joseph simply to a truthful first-century Bill Clinton: "He did not have sexual relations with that woman." There's much more to be said. Joseph is not Jesus's biological father, but he is his *real* father. In his adoption of Jesus, Joseph is rightly identified by the Spirit speaking through the Scriptures as Jesus's father (Luke 2:41, 48).

Jesus would have said, "*Abba*" first to Joseph.

Jesus's obedience to his father and mother, obedience essential to his law keeping on our behalf, is directed toward Joseph (Luke 2:51). Jesus does not share Joseph's bloodline, but he claims him as his father, obeying Joseph perfectly and even following in his vocation. When Jesus is tempted in the wilderness, he cites the words of Deuteronomy to counter "the flaming darts of the evil one" (Eph. 6:16). Think about it for a moment—Jesus almost certainly learned those Hebrew Scriptures from Joseph as he listened to him at the woodworking table or stood beside him in the synagogue.

And, perhaps most significantly, if Joseph is *not* "really" the father of Jesus, you and I are going to hell.

Jesus's identity as the Christ, after all, is tied to his identity as the descendant of David, the legitimate heir to David's throne. Jesus saves us as David's son, the offspring of Abraham, the Christ. That human identity came to Jesus through adoption. Matthew and Luke trace Jesus's roots in Abraham and David through the line of Joseph. As the Presbyterian scholar J. Gresham Machen put it, Joseph's adoption of Jesus means Jesus belongs "to the house of David just as truly as if he were in a physical sense the son of Joseph. He was a gift of God to the Davidic house, not less truly, but on the contrary in a more wonderful way than if he had been descended from David by ordinary generation."[2] It is through Joseph that Jesus finds his identity as the fulfillment of the Old Testament promise. It is through Joseph's legal fatherhood of Jesus that "the hopes and fears of all the years" find their realization in the final son of Abraham, son of David, and son of Israel.

Joseph Reflects the Image of God

Joseph's fatherhood is significant for us precisely because of the way the gospel anchors it to the fatherhood of God himself. Joseph marries the virgin girl, taking the responsibility for the baby on himself. Moreover, he protects the woman and her child by rescuing them from

Herod's sword, exiling them in Egypt until the dictator's rampage was ended by death. Interestingly, Matthew tells us, "This was to fulfill what the Lord had spoken by the prophet, 'Out of Egypt I called my son'" (Matt. 2:15). Now, at first glance this seems to be an embarrassing error on the part of the apostle. After all, the Scripture passage he references—from Hosea 11:1—isn't about something in the future but about something in the past. "When Israel was a child, I loved him, and out of Egypt I called my son," God declares in the past tense, speaking of the exodus of the Israelites from Egypt. Isn't Matthew misinterpreting the plain reading of the Bible? No.

Israel, remember, is being called out to bring forth the blessing to the nations, the Christ of God. Israel is the "son" of God precisely because of her relationship to the Christ who is to come. God, in the exodus, is preparing his people for a final exodus to come in Christ. Jesus sums up in his life the history of Israel and the history of the world, living out this history in obedient trust of his Father. He then fulfills the flight out of Egypt in the same way he fulfills the march into the Promised Land: the promises find their yes and their amen in him, the shadows find their substance in him. It's not that Jesus is the copy of Israel coming out of Egypt, but that Israel coming out of Egypt was the copy—in advance—of Jesus.[3]

Israel wound up in Egypt the first time through violence. The brothers of Israel sought to kill a young dreamer named Joseph. God, though, meant it for good, using the sojourn in Egypt to protect the nation from famine (Gen. 50:20). The Joseph of old told his brothers, "I will provide for you and your little ones" (Gen. 50:21). Joseph of Nazareth pictures his namesake in providing for and protecting Jesus in Egypt. But he also pictures God, the One who brought the people in and out of Egypt, who shields them from the dictator's murderous conspiracies.

Joseph is unique in one sense. He is called to provide for and protect the Christ of God. But in other ways Joseph is not unique at all. All of us, as followers of Christ, are called to protect children. And protecting children doesn't simply mean saving their lives—although it certainly means that—or providing for their material needs—although, again, it does mean that. Governments are called to protect the innocent and to punish evildoers (Rom. 13:1–5), which is why we should work to outlaw abortion, infanticide, child abuse, and other threats to children. Governments and private agencies can play a role in providing economic relief to the impoverished, which is why Christians weigh in on issues such as divorce policy, labor laws, and welfare reform.

The Fatherhood of God

But picturing the fatherhood of God means more than these things. His fatherhood is personal, familial. Protecting children means rolling back the curse of fatherlessness, inasmuch as it lies within our power to do so.

When parents care for a child—their child—they're picturing something bigger than themselves. They are an icon of a cosmic reality—the reality of the Father "from whom every family in heaven and on earth is named" (Eph. 3:15).

Joseph's rescue of Jesus isn't the first time the adoption of a child is tied to the exodus event. David sings about God as "Father of the fatherless and protector of widows" who "settles the solitary in a home," tying this reality to God marching before his people through the wilderness toward Canaan (Ps. 68:5–6). God shows this is the kind of God he is. He's the kind of God, the prophet Hosea tells us, of whom we cry out, "In you the orphan finds mercy" (Hos. 14:3).

God everywhere tells us he is seeking to reclaim the marred image of himself in humanity by conforming us to the image of Christ who is the image of the invisible God. As we become Christlike, we become godly. As we become godly, we grow in holiness—differentness from the age around us. This God-imaging holiness means, therefore, an imaging of God's affections, including his love for orphans. After delivering Israel from Egypt and speaking to them from the mountain of Sinai, God tells his people to be like him. "He executes justice for the fatherless and the widow, and loves the sojourner, giving him food and clothing," God says through Moses. "Love the sojourner, therefore, for you were sojourners in the land of Egypt" (Deut. 10:18–19).

You might hear some criticize the Bible as "patriarchal." If by this they mean the Bible is about propping up male privilege or self-interest, they're wrong. If they mean the Bible sanctions the abuse of women or denies the dignity and equality of women, they're wrong. But depending on how one defines patriarchy, they're correct that the Bible is patriarchal. The ancient world's concept of patriarchy, after all, wasn't so much about who was "in charge," in the way we tend to think of it, although the father of a family was clearly the head of that family. In the biblical picture, though, the father is responsible to bear the burden of providing for and protecting his family.

When God creates the first human beings, he commands them to "be fruitful and multiply" (Gen. 1:28) and builds into them unique characteristics to carry out this task. The Creator designs the woman to bring forth and nurture offspring. Her name, Eve, means, the Scriptures tell us, "the mother of all living" (Gen. 3:20). The cosmic curse that comes upon the creation shows up, for the woman, in the pain through which she carries out this calling—birth pangs (Gen. 3:16). The man, as the first human father, is "to work the ground from which he was taken" (Gen. 3:23). Adam, made of earth, is to bring forth bread from the earth, a calling that is also frustrated by the curse (Gen. 3:17–19). In this, Adam images a Father who protects and provides for his children.

Thus, Jesus teaches us to pray to a Father who grants us "daily bread" (Matt. 6:11). He points to the natural inclination of a father to give to his son a piece of bread or a fish as an icon of the patriarchy of God: "If you then, who are evil, know how to give good gifts to your children, how much more will your Father who is in heaven give good things to those who ask him" (Matt. 7:11).

Indeed, the apostle Paul charges any father who refuses to provide for his family with being "worse than an unbeliever" (1 Tim. 5:8). In fact, Paul says that such a man has already "denied the faith." Why? It is precisely because being in Christ means recognition of the fatherhood of God. The abandoning or neglectful father blasphemes against such divine fatherhood with a counter-portrayal that is not true to the blessed reality.

Burdens of Parenting

Parenting means sacrifice. It seems that every couple of years someone comes out with a psychological or sociological study showing that parents have higher levels of anxiety and depression than those without children. I don't dispute those studies at all. The question, though, is why is there such anxiety, such sadness, in the lives of parents?

I hope I don't succumb to the sin of anxiety or lack of trust in God. But I do worry about my sons. I hope for the best for them. I feel the weight of my example before them. Before I became a father, I felt conviction of sin when I snapped at someone, but I never felt the depression that comes with realizing that I've snapped at one of *my sons*. I feel sorry for a young man who's been rejected by the woman he thought was meant to be his wife, but I've never cried about it. I can imagine myself weeping behind closed doors, though, if it ever happened to my son Timothy. I've always loathed child molesters and raged against the way the courts and churches so often coddle them. But I've never had my blood pressure accelerate the way it does when a suspicious-acting, creepily friendly man kneels to talk to my kids. Having a baby yanks one into a whole new world of responsibility for the shaping of a life, a family, a future.

That kind of anxiety isn't limited to parents within a household. We can also see the same thing in the "fathers" and "mothers" within the church, those who love the gathered believers with a love that cherishes, and aches, like that of a parent.

The apostle Paul writes of his "toil . . . night and day" over the church at Thessalonica because he loved them "like a nursing mother taking care of her own children" (1 Thess. 2:7–9). One can sense the gravity of emotion when the apostle John warns the churches with the urgency of a father, "Little children, keep yourselves from idols" (1 John 5:21)—just like a mom who calls out, "Johnny! Stay away from that electrical wire!"

It's easy, though, not to feel this. A certain kind of manufactured calm can come to those who don't wish to be parents or who abandon their children to the welfare state or to the abortionist's sword. This kind of freedom doesn't startle you out of a midnight slumber or cause you to run anxious hands through your hair in frustration. No one is watching to see how you trained up a new generation to worship or spurn the God of your fathers.

But what an impoverished sense of pseudo-*shalom* this must be. It's the peace of a beggar who is content to glean from the fields while never risking the possibility of failing as a farmer. There's a high price for such peace.

Every night I lay my hands on the head of my five sons and pray for the salvation of Benjamin, Timothy, Samuel, Jonah, and Taylor. I pray they'll be godly men of courage and conviction. I pray God will give them godly wives (one apiece) and that he would spare them from rebellious teenage years and from the horror of divorce.

And when I'm really aware of my responsibility, I pray they'll be good dads. Yes, I pray for the salvation of the world, for healed marriages across the board. But not like this. They're my boys. And sometimes when I think about the alternative to their salvation, there's a sawing ache I never knew as a single man looking at a world map. There's a sense of my own helplessness—and my own possible failure—that never kept me awake at night in a college dormitory room.

I guess you could call that burden depressing—sometimes it is. I suppose you could track it on a chart as anxiety. And I suppose you could avoid that depression, that anxiety, by seeking to feed only your own mouth, to be held responsible for only your own life, or just yours and a spouse's. But what if in so doing, you're protecting yourself from more than possible sadness and grief? What if you're protecting yourself from love?

Doing as Our Heavenly Father

God is not anxious. God isn't depressed. But God's fatherhood is pictured for us as a tumultuous, fighting kind of fatherhood—the kind that rips open the seas and drowns armies. Joseph probably had no idea that he was a living reenactment of the deliverance of Israel from Egypt. He probably never thought about the fact he was serving as an icon of his God. He just did what seemed right, in obedience to the Word of God. But he was participating in something dramatic—in every sense of the word.

When we adopt—and when we encourage a culture of adoption in our churches and communities—we're picturing something that's true about our God. We, like Jesus, see what our Father is doing and do likewise (John 5:19). And what our Father is doing, it turns out, is fighting for orphans, making them sons and daughters.

3

Adoption and the Walk of Faith

Our contemporary cartoonish, two-dimensional picture of Joseph too easily ignores how difficult it was for him to do what he did. Imagine for a minute that one of the teenagers in your church were to stand up behind the pulpit to give her testimony. She's eight months pregnant and unmarried. After a few minutes of talking about God's working in her life and about how excited she is to be a mother, she starts talking about how thankful she is that she's remained sexually pure, kept all the "True Love Waits" commitments she made in her youth group Bible study, and is glad to announce that she's still a virgin. You'd immediately conclude that the girl is either delusional or lying.

When contemporary biblical revisionists scoff at the virgin birth of Jesus and other miracles, they often tell us we're now beyond such "myths" since we live in a post-Enlightenment, scientifically progressive information age. What such critics miss is the fact that virgin conceptions have always seemed ridiculous. People in first-century Palestine knew how babies were conceived. The implausibility of the whole thing is evident in the biblical text itself. When Mary tells Joseph she is pregnant, his first reaction isn't a cheery "It's beginning to look a lot like Christmas." No, he assumes what any of us would conclude was going on, and he sets out to end their betrothal.

But then God enters the scene.

When God speaks in a dream to Joseph about the identity of Jesus, Joseph, like everyone who follows Christ, recognizes the voice and goes forward (Matt. 1:21–24). Joseph's adoption and protection of Jesus is simply the outworking of that belief.

In believing God, Joseph probably walks away from his reputation. The wags in his hometown would probably always whisper about how "poor Joseph was hoodwinked by that girl" or how "old Joseph got himself in trouble with that girl." As the stakes get higher, Joseph certainly walks away from his economic security. In first-century Galilee, after all, one doesn't simply move to Egypt, the way one might today decide to move to New York or London. Joseph surrenders a household economy, a vocation probably built up over generations, handed down to him, one would suppose, by his father.

Genuine Faith

Again, Joseph was unique in one sense. None of us will ever be called to be father to God. But in another very real sense, Joseph's faith was exactly the same as ours. The letter of James, for instance, speaks of the definition of faith in this way: "Religion that is pure and undefiled before God, the Father, is this: to visit orphans and widows in their affliction, and to keep oneself unstained from the world" (1:27). James is the one who tells us further that faith is not mere intellectual belief, the faith of demons (2:19), but is instead a faith that works.

James shows us that Abraham's belief is seen in his offering up Isaac, knowing God would keep his promise and raise him from the dead (2:21–23). We know Rahab has faith not simply because she raises her hand in agreement with the Hebrew spies but because in hiding them from the enemy she is showing she trusts God to save her (2:25). James tells us that genuine faith shelters the orphan.

What gives even more weight to these words is the identity of the human author. This letter is written by James of the Jerusalem church, the brother of our Lord Jesus.[4] How much of this "pure and undefiled religion" did James see first in the life of his own earthly father? Did the image of Joseph linger in James's mind as he inscribed the words of an orphan-protecting, living faith?

Not long ago I sat in a coffee shop with a friend and former student, now a faithful pastor, hearing how things were moving along in his congregation. He talked about various mission projects within the church, including a yearly mission trip to an overseas orphanage to care for the children there and to help connect them with adopting parents. Some folks in the church, my pastor friend said, wanted to discontinue the orphanage work in order to do something, as they put it, "more evangelistic." A group of faithful Christians have been serving orphans—helping place them in Christian homes where they'll grow up with the gospel— and some feel guilty for not doing something "evangelistic"! That's a tragedy. What better way is there to bring the good news of Christ than to see his unwanted little brothers and sisters placed in families where they'll be raised in the nurture and admonition of the Lord?

Because genuine faith is orphan protecting, a culture of adoption and a culture of evangelism coexist together. Indeed they grow from the same root. Christians who counsel pregnant women and who staff orphanages and who help families adopt aren't "social welfare people" as opposed to the "soul-winning people" in the next pew.

A Countercultural Choice

A few years ago, the Presiding Bishop of the Episcopal Church USA kicked up a stir of controversy with comments in a national newsmagazine, differentiating mainline Episcopalians from more theologically conservative groups such as Roman Catholics and evangelical Protestants. In her view, Episcopalians "tend to be better educated and tend to reproduce at lower rates than some other denominations." Episcopalians, she said, "encourage people to pay attention to the stewardship of the earth and not use more than their portion."[5]

Well, she's right, of course. Mainline Episcopalians in this country do tend to be well-educated and affluent, and the homeschooling mom with six kids in tow in the line at the grocery store in front of you is not likely to be an Episcopalian. But what about those "other denominations" the bishop mentioned? What about those of us whose communions are less well-educated and who have, as she put it, "theological reasons for producing lots of children"?

My denomination was once seen as one of the most aggressively evangelistic groups on the planet. Some of you may have similar stories about your denominations and churches, and maybe you've seen the same kind of trajectory. In my grandfather's day, conservative evangelicals were often derided by American culture as redneck and backward. There's still hostility toward evangelical Christianity in certain sectors of American life, of course, but evangelical Christians are now invited to the Rotary Club meetings. We're being elected to Congress. People now at least pretend to know how to respond to our evangelistic tracts in order to get our votes for President of the United States. We're not in the trailer parks anymore. Our young men are successful, suburban, and career minded—and our young women are too. Like the rest of American culture, we often see children as something expected but to be minimized, lest they get in the way of our dreams. And we think that's a sign of health.

Meanwhile our baptisms go down, and our birthrates do too. It turns out that keeping up with the Episcopalians can have a downside.

Churches that don't celebrate children aren't going to celebrate evangelism. After all, the "be fruitful and multiply" clause in Genesis is echoed in the Great Commission of Jesus (Matt. 28:16–20), a mission that also seeks to fill the entire earth. Jesus links procreation to new creation by speaking of new converts as newborn babies and of conversion itself as a new birth. When Jesus stands before his Father with the redeemed of all the ages, he will announce us as "the children God has given me" (Heb. 2:13).

Churches that mimic (even if by default, with silence) the culture's view that life is about possessions or sentimental pop-music romance or self-advancement simply aren't going to produce men and women committed to giving up these things for the cause of global evangelism and missions. Faithful Christian congregations must be distinct from the blob spirituality of

47

contemporary Western civilization. And what is more countercultural than the embrace of children as gifts from a good Lord? We live in an era when a mom with five children receives snide comments, even from her children's pediatrician ("Don't you know what's causing that?"). A congregation that exults in new life, from the pulpit and from the pew, is a congregation that's going to cause onlookers to ask why.

If the people in our congregation become other-directed instead of self-directed in the adoption of unwanted children, they are going to be other-directed instead of self-directed in their verbal witness to people in their community. On the other hand, the same self-interest that sears over the joy of birth will sear over the joy of the new birth. The numbness to earthly adoption is easily translated to numbness to spiritual adoption. But if people in our churches learn not to grumble at the blessing of minivans filled with children—some of whom don't look anything alike—they're going to learn not to grumble at the blessing of a congregation filling with new people, some of whom don't look anything alike. If our churches learn to rejoice in newness of life in the church nursery, they'll more easily rejoice at newness of life in the church baptistery, and vice versa.

This doesn't mean that we should equate fertility (or prolific adoption) with spirituality. God calls many believers not to marry so that, like the apostle Paul, they can devote themselves totally to Great Commission service. Others will not be blessed with large families or with children at all. We must insist on the church as a household, not as a collection of family units. But at the same time, can't we insist that our view of children be dictated by the book of Proverbs rather than by Madison Avenue or Wall Street?

Unbridled capitalist prosperity doesn't make love, babies, or societies. It certainly doesn't build a church. What we need is a vision that transcends our gnawing after what we think we want and need. We need a vision that shows us that a person's life "does not consist in the abundance of his possessions" (Luke 12:15).

Seeking first the kingdom of God, as Jesus tells us to do (Matt. 6:33), means recognizing what kind of kingdom we're seeking. When we pray "Your kingdom come," we're asking that "your will be done, on earth as it is in heaven" (Matt. 6:10). When the psalmist cries out for that kingdom to come, he pleads, "Give justice to the weak and the fatherless; maintain the right of the afflicted and the destitute" (Ps. 82:3).

The kingdom of Christ is characterized in Scripture as a kingdom of rescued children. Solomon looks to the final reign of God's anointed and sings, "For he delivers the needy when he calls, the poor and him who has no helper. He has pity on the weak and the needy, and saves the lives of the needy. From oppression and violence he redeems their life, and precious is their blood in his sight" (Ps. 72:12–14). When we protect and welcome children, we're announcing something about Jesus and his kingdom.

If that characterizes the kingdom to come, then why aren't our churches—which are, after all, outposts of that rule of Jesus—characterized by it now? When we recognize the face of Jesus reflected in faces we may never see until the resurrection—those of the vulnerable unborn and unwanted—we're doing more than cultural activism. We are contending for the faith once for all delivered to the saints (Jude 3).

An orphan-protecting adoption culture is countercultural—and always has been. Some of the earliest records we have of the Christian churches speak of how Christians, remarkably, protected children in the face of a culture of death pervasive in the Roman Empire. The followers of Jesus, though, did not kill their offspring, even when it would have made economic or social sense to do so.[6] This is still distinctively Christian in a world that increasingly sees children as, at best, a commodity to be controlled and, at worst, a nuisance to be contained. Think of how revolutionary it is for Christians to adopt a young boy with a cleft palate from a region of India where most people see him as "defective." Think of how counterintuitive it is for Christians to adopt a Chinese girl—when many there see her as a disappointment. Think of how odd it must seem to American secularists to see Christians adopting a baby whose body trembles with an addiction to the cocaine her mother sent through her bloodstream before birth. Think of the kind of credibility such action lends to the proclamation of our gospel.

Advancing the Cause of Physical and Spiritual Life

An adoption culture in our churches advances the cause of life, even beyond the individual lives of the children adopted. Imagine if Christian churches were known as the places where unwanted babies become beloved children. If this were the case across the board around the world, sure, there would still be abortions, there would still be abusive homes. But wouldn't we see more women willing to give their children life if they'd seen with their own eyes what an adoption culture looks like? And wouldn't these mothers and fathers, who may themselves feel unwanted, be a bit more ready to hear our talk about a kingdom where all are welcomed? The contemporary Planned Parenthood movement was started by a woman named Margaret Sanger, who defended abortion rights on the basis of eugenics, the search for "good genes" based on the racist and evolutionary notions of "social Darwinism" prevalent in her day. Sanger's grandson, Alexander, continues her viewpoint, updated with contemporary notions of sociobiology, in virulent opposition to the viability of an adoption culture—on Darwinist grounds. "Adoption is counter-intuitive from an evolutionary vantage point of both the biological mother and the adoptive parents," Sanger argues. "Adoption requires a person to devote time and resources to raising a child that is not genetically related. Adoption also puts the future of a child in the control of a stranger."[7] It's easier for a woman to have an abortion, Sanger argues, or for a family to refuse to think about adopting, because evolution and biology "conspire to thwart adoption. Evolution has programmed women to be nurturers of the children they bear."[8] That's why, the abortion industry heir contends, adoption "as the 'solution' to the abortion problem is a cruel hoax."[9]

Sanger has an ideology, a family heritage, and the financial viability of the abortion industry to guard; so his words aren't going to convince many followers of Jesus. But aren't they sad, and telling?

Perhaps what our churches need most of all in our defense of the faith against Darwinian despair is not more resources on how the fossil record fits with the book of Genesis and not more arguments on how molecular structures show evidence of design. Perhaps the most practical way your congregation can show Darwinism to be wrong is to showcase families for whom love is more than gene protection.

Orphan-Protecting Faith
Despite Personal Hurt

As with Joseph, this orphan-protecting faith is personal as well as corporate. At the judgment seat of Christ, all of us will be evaluated as to the authenticity of our faith on the basis of our reaction to "the least of these" (Matt. 25:31–46). At first blush, this looks like works-righteousness, the very kind of thing away from which the rest of the Bible is calling us. You might wonder, if we're judged on this basis, then shouldn't each of us adopt as many children as we have square footage in our homes—and then buy more square footage? No. The remarkable thing about Jesus's revelation about the judgment seat is that neither the "sheep" (those who inherit the kingdom) nor the "goats" (those who inherit hell) seem to know what Jesus is talking about. When Jesus tells the righteous they sheltered and fed and clothed him in his distress, they ask, "Lord, when did we . . ." (Matt. 25:37). And when Jesus tells the unrighteous they refused to do such things, they also ask, "Lord, when did we . . ." (Matt. 25:44).

At issue isn't a list of righteous deeds. At issue is whether Jesus knows us, whether we are "blessed" by the Father (Matt. 25:34). The faith that sees Christ presented in the gospel sees Christ in his brothers when they appear providentially in the life of the believer. Jesus tells us there will always be people who appeal to their knowledge of the King, their "personal relationship to Jesus." Do they recognize him, though, apart from his sky-exploding glory? Do they see the covert Christ in the suffering of the vulnerable?

Not every believer will stand praying outside an abortion clinic. Not every believer will take a pregnant teenager into his or her guest bedroom. Not every believer is called to adopt children. But every believer is called to recognize Jesus in the face of his little brothers and sisters when he decides to show up in their lives, even if it interrupts everything else.

The judgment of this kind of faith is intensely personal. A few years ago a group of us were riveted as we listened to Billy Graham at a crusade in Indianapolis preaching on final judgment. The evangelist told the crowd that many of them mistakenly thought of the judgment to come in the same way they think of the Indianapolis 500 car race—as a great mass of people milling around together. "You think you'll be there with all your friends, drinking beer," Graham said. "But you're wrong. When you stand in judgment, you'll stand *alone*." The evangelist was old and weak. His voice was shaky, and he had to be helped to the podium, hardly the fiery preacher of the mid-twentieth century. But when the crowd heard the word *alone*, in that famous Carolina mountain accent, there was almost a chill in the stadium. In the judgment to come, our faith will lie exposed before the eyes of our God, and there will be nowhere to hide.

Thousands of years ago, a man named Job recognized that his own judgment would have to do with his treatment of orphans. In the book of Job, the suffering man told God that he would neither withhold food or raise his hand against the fatherless (Job 31:16–22). Job said instead that "from my youth the fatherless grew up with me as with a father, and from my mother's womb I guided the widow" (Job 31:18). Why was this so? Job said, "For I was in terror of calamity from God, and I could not have faced his majesty" (Job 31:23).

Joseph of Nazareth could resonate with Job's plea. Joseph easily could have walked out to the city gates, shaking his head to his friends. "You'll never believe the crazy dream I had last night." He no doubt would have denounced everywhere Herod's pagan insanity in killing babies and toddlers. No one would have blamed him for putting aside his betrothal to Mary. In fact, he probably would have been praised at his funeral for his kindness in not calling for her to be stoned to death. Joseph could have married a pious Jewish woman, could have fathered several of his "own" children. He could have slept easily at night, perhaps, and then died an old man. No one would have thought him to be evil or even negligent. But if he'd done that, he would have been standing with the spirit of Antichrist rather than with the Spirit of Christ. No one else was called to adopt this Christ-child, but he was. And because he believed his God, he obeyed him, even to his own hurt.

Joseph's faith was the same kind of faith that saves us. Very few, if any, of us will have a dream directing us to adopt a child. None of us will be directed to do what Joseph did—to teach Jesus Christ how to saw through wood or to recite Deuteronomy in Hebrew. But all of us are called to be compassionate. All of us are called to remember the poor. All of us are called to remember the fatherless and the widows. That will look different in our different lives, with the different situations and resources God has given us. But for all of us there'll be a judgment to test the genuineness of our faith. And for some of us, there'll be some orphan faces there.

Conclusion

What's at Stake When We
Talk about Adoption

It's a shame that Joseph is so neglected in our thoughts and affections, even at Christmastime. If we pay attention to him, though, we just might see a model for a new generation of Christians. We might see how to live as the presence of Christ in a culture of death. We might see how to image a protective Father and how to preach a life-affirming gospel, even in a culture captivated by the spirit of Herod.

If we follow in the way of Joseph, perhaps we'll see a battalion of new church-sponsored clinics for pregnant women in crisis situations (and I word it this way because, as a dear friend rightly reminds me, there are no "crisis pregnancies"). Perhaps we'll train God-called women in our churches to counsel confused young women, counselors able and equipped to provide an alternative to the slick but deadly propaganda of the abortion profiteers. If we walk in Joseph's way, perhaps we'll see pastors who will prophetically call on Christians to oppose the death culture by rescuing babies and children through adoption.

Think of the plight of the orphan somewhere right now out there in the world. It's not just that she's lonely. It's that she has no inheritance, no future. With every passing year, she's less "cute," less adoptable. In just a few years, on her eighteenth birthday, she'll be expelled from the orphanage or from "the system." What will happen to her then? Maybe she'll join the military or find some job training. Maybe she'll stare at a tile on the ceiling above her as her body is violated by a man who's willing to pay her enough to eat for a day, alone in a back alley or in front of a camera crew of strangers. Maybe she'll place a revolver in her mouth or tie a rope around her neck, knowing no one will have to deal with her except, once again, the bureaucratic "authorities" who can clean up the mess she leaves behind. Can you feel the force of such desperation? Jesus can. She's his little sister.

What if a mighty battalion of Christian parents would open their hearts and their homes to unwanted infants—infants some so-called "clinics" would like to see carried out with the medical waste? It might mean that next Christmas there'll be one more stocking at the chimney at your house—a new son or daughter who escaped the abortionist's knife or the orphanage's grip to find at your knee the grace of a carpenter's Son.

Planned Parenthood thinks "Choice on Earth" is the message of Christmas, and perhaps it is in a Christmas culture more identified with shopping malls than with churches. But we know better, or at least we should. Let's follow the footsteps of the other man at the manger, the quiet one. And as we read the proclamation of the shepherds, exploding in the sky as a declaration of war, let's remind a miserable generation there are some things more joyous than choice—things like peace and life and love.

Notes

1. I am indebted to my friend David Prince for this observation, which he preached to his congregation at Ashland Avenue Baptist Church in Lexington, Kentucky.
2. J. Gresham Machen, *The Virgin Birth of Christ* (New York: Harper, 1930), 129.
3. For a helpful discussion of how Jesus fulfills the "out of Egypt" prophecy, see John Murray, "The Unity of the Old and New Testaments," in *Collected Writings of John Murray: The Claims of Truth*, vol. 1 (Edinburgh: Banner of Truth, 1976), 25–26.
4. For a detailed discussion of the identity of James and his relationship to Jesus, see Douglas J. Moo, *The Letter of James*, Pillar New Testament Commentary (Grand Rapids, MI: Eerdmans, 2000), 11–22. I agree with Moo's assessment that the author of the letter of James is indeed our Lord's brother, per the traditional view.
5. Deborah Solomon, "State of the Church: Questions for Katharine Jefferts Schori," *New York Times*, November 19, 2006, 21.
6. "The Epistle to Diognetus," in *The Apostolic Fathers: Greek Texts and English Translations*, trans. Michael W. Holmes, 3rd. ed. (Grand Rapids, MI: Baker, 2007), 703.
7. Alexander Sanger, *Beyond Choice: Reproductive Freedom in the 21st Century* (New York: Public Affairs, 2004), 142.
8. Ibid., 143.
9. Ibid., 144.

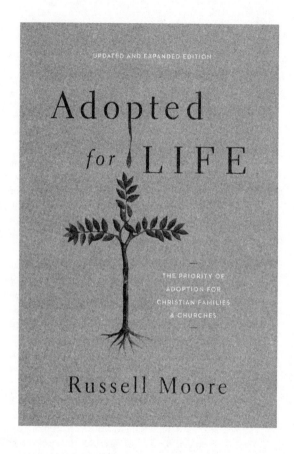